In *Finding the Well*, Corky (Kathleen) Culver rows down rivers and across lakes, admires fibonacci patterns in turtles and sago palms, recalls protest marches and the parties afterwards. Throughout, she voices no regrets: long-ago affairs, arthritic joints, mosquito bites are all grist for poetry, for incantations and blessings (let dancers dance, let all / talents aching for outlet / find them). In these dispatches from an unapologetically "rowdy hag," we're immersed in a chronicle of a woman's life, a woman's body, a woman's loves. —**Rosalie Morales Kearns**, author of the novel Kingdom of Women (Jaded Ibis), editor of the short story anthology The Female Complaint: Tales of Unruly Women (Shade Mountain)

Finding the Well traces a recursive path within a remarkable range. Whether touching down beside the tidepools of the West Coast, in the deep caverns of Florida's springs, at protest marches, or inside intimate moments, Culver's poems chime with lyrical notes, the natural world, and universal concerns. Her profound delight in the pleasure of language and her generous imagination invoke bright human possibilities, promising that even when we're subject to limits, "we will be understudies / of the fire opal where, in its confined / space, colors dance and swirl." These are poems for falling in love, for celebrations, and for moments of "floundering in the bardo," bringing intelligence and compassion to life on the page. —**Michele Sharpe**, author of the memoir, *Walk Away* (Kindle) and poetry collection, *Back East* (Moon Pie Press), winner of the 2013 Macklin Prize.

The resplendent poetry of Kathleen Culver is set deep in the glories of Florida's natural world where a river "relaxes toward the ocean" and "frog eggs attach to grasses/secure enough to wait and watch." Culver writes of aging, "Time, you slippery freak . . ." and of the women, where "lovers turn into ex-lovers then/into friends, and friends/turn to life-long loves." Even in the poem "Early in the Virus Years," her signature gentle humor persists. "My spouse has ordered a bidet and an ice cream maker." From her childhood eighty years ago to today—"we see fascism coming, watch it spin in the air"—*Finding the Well*, this second collection of Culver's poetry, allows us intimate access into the life journey of a poet. —**Sandra Gail Lambert**, author of the memoir *A Certain Loneliness*

Finding the Well

Other Poetry by Kathleen Culver

Natural Law of Water, 2007

Finding the Well
Kathleen Culver

Copyright © 2022 Kathleen Culver

First Edition 2022.

All rights reserved. This book may not be reproduced in part or in whole by any means without written permission from the Publisher, except for in the case of brief quotations embodied in critical articles and reviews. For more information, contact Circledance Books, PO Box 1863, Melrose, FL 32666 or sisorbit@windstream.net.

Some of these poems have been previously published in the same form or in an earlier version in *Wild Roof Journal, Tipping the Scales, Otherworldly Women Press, Showbear Family Circus, Halcyone/Black Mtn. Press/HerWords, Rogue Agent, The Thing Itself, Sinister Wisdom*

ISBN: 979-8-9858000-0-5

Acknowledgements

Much thanks to my poetry group - Susan, Samara, Aliesa, Jenna, Feral, and especially Michele - whose feedback and inspiration made this book possible. Sweetest memories of Barbara Davis whose encouragement and transcriptions from the start were greatly appreciated. Finally, my gratitude to Marie Steinwachs who helped smooth the rough edges and bring this book into fruition.

Contents

ICHETUCKNEE CANOE

Santa Fe Day 1
Fog Song 2
Journal at Silver Glen Spring 4
River Communities 5
Gulf Island Ceremonial 6
Speechless 8
Big Island Ballet 10
Ichetucknee Canoe 12
Lake Morning 13
Brook Farms 14
A New Sunflower Species 15
Cavern 16
Greens of August 17
I See You, But So What 18
Today's Tropical Adrenaline 19
Old Women and the Weeds 20
Vultures and Winter Rye 21
Freeze Forecast in a Blue Moon 22
Winter Dawn 23
Ravine Ritual 24
Ripening 25
Yellow Fly Season 26
Three Generations Clearing Weeds from the Lake 28
Cold Snap 30

SQUASH BLOSSOM SUMMER

Untitled 33

Food of an Affair 34

Kentucky Bourbon 36

Platonic 37

Kissing Cousins 38

Body Surfing 40

Couple Seeks Geographical Cure 42

September Bardo 43

Zombie Love 44

'Bye Sug 45

Divorce 46

Sailor's Farewell 47

Sticking Points 48

Not Medusa 50

Midsummer Night's Eve 51

On the Verge 52

After Mallarmé 53

Breakup in November 54

These Days with Us 56

In Love Again 57

Poem for Pat 58

Saucerie 60

Haiku 61

SAGO AND SPIRALS

The Point of Palms 63

Solstice and the Changing Seen 64

Triptych 66
Life on a Pedestal 67
Art After 68
Anne Sexton Dream 69
My One and Only Poem to Charles Bukowski 70
Valentine to a Poet 71
Rash Diagnosis and Diogenes's Lamp 72
I Want to Be Worthy: A Sermon for Self 74
Time, You're a Rowdy Hag Like Me 76
Beware All-Consuming Passions 77
Vespers 78
Sleep Tight 79
One Shoe 80
The Journals of Lost Brothers 81
Holy Day USA 82
Pi Day 83
Silver Delicious 84
Aging with You 85
Vernal Equinox 86
Twelve 88
Break Out 89
Keeping Up Appearances 90
Palaces of the Poor 92
How to Tell if You're a Poet 94

TRAVEL TALES

Drought At Goldhead 95
Solo Roads and the Single Girl 96

Ode to Heat 98

Poet at an Outdoor Restaurant 101

A Pilgrimage to See Sister Maggie................................ 102

Don't Take the Subway Today 104

Travel Tales 13, A Shipboard Romance 106

Afterwards 109

Moving to Hollywood.. 110

Aging Wing Walker 111

Just a Second 112

Youth at the Gallery of Medieval Knights, New York Metropolitan Museum, 1960................................... 113

Atlas on the Cruise Ship Ryndam 114

Beachdaze – do wah, de water, do whatcha like......... 116

Detroit behind the Eight Ball 118

Mystic on the Tarmac 119

Sea Lion Lines 120

Trip 123

Arcade: Quarter in Hand I Approach Her 124

Visitor 126

MEMOIR FROM THE REVOLUTION

Memoir from the Revolution.. 127

How to Stop Fascism... 128

Alabama, 1961... 130

Oh to Iron Out the Ironies 131

Year of Strong Storms 132

Evil Visible Again 134

Election 136

Moment in Congress	137
Vilano Beach	138
Secrets of Success	139
Politics and the Little People	140
Covid Cancellation	142
Shutdown Carnegie Hall and other Caverns	143
Lost Parties	144
After the Protest	145
Early in the Virus Years	146
Voices in the Chorus of Millions---2020	148
Ancestors	150
Our, a Love Poem for Humanity	152

Ichetucknee Canoe

Santa Fe Day

The river relaxes toward the ocean
does not need a sense of purpose
just allows the flow.
Frog eggs attach to grasses
secure enough to wait and hatch,
a fat beaver snoozes on the bank,
turtles warm in the sun, though
if the canoe comes close,
they'll splash off the log into the dark
wet cool.

The ease seems eternal, steady, unending,
flowing around our fingers.
We don't want to imagine
the current will ever run out,
this rusty-colored water with amber beams,
offering us itself.

Cypress knees gather around the river spirit
like monks, dragonflies grace our knees,
and light stills speech. The peace
we asked for, we have for now.

Fog Song

At dawn
you may take a boat

out on the lake
and be

surprised by fog
enveloping you so

you lose track of
where you are.

No shores
no direction clear.

It's just you and
your soul.

Put the oars on
the gunnels,

feel the small rocking
of the water,

the shifts without
compass,

afloat in a cloud
moist gray,

almost a caress,
almost a kindness.

Listen to the song
of quiet.

Journal at Silver Glen Spring

In the open pool you see grays, silver, aqua,
then the deepest color over the deepest part
a blue that stops breath
impossible to describe.

The spring's opening is there
between two slopes. Above,
a brow of smooth sand and
at the mouth, the lower slope
covered with small white shells
up from the aquifer, gradually
worked free from being embedded
in limestone seabeds
of the Pleistocene.

Here the spring fountains forth, offering
pure, clear water, and sometimes,
one would think, advice,
to see the fish and humans
line up before it, quieted, attentive.

River Communities

Monkeys living alongside the Silver River
enjoy a waterside view, often pick a fallen
tree as a perfect porch, or a nice limb
now and then where they can perch
while a friend grooms their back.
Sometimes a baby clinging to a belly
is carried high in the tree to munch
peeled tips of new twigs.

Turtles prefer rocks and snags
out in the water, possibly to avoid
pestering monkeys, certainly to get
double heat of sun and reflections,
while they bask. Canoes and kayaks
are advised to take their pauses on
snags as well, because a monkey just might
jump aboard if they come too close.

Boaters call out tips to one another,
*otters ahead, big alligator, swimming hole
for the bold.* We are grateful for the
privilege of being here, trying not to think of
how towns and lawns and ranches and dairy farms
greedily gulp the river,
the human habit of destroying habitats.

Gulf Island Ceremonial

We paddle a narrow path
through saw grass's sharp blades
lashing at our arms, arrive
at the beach, and a quick swim in clothes,
saltwater burning, then cooling
our slashed skin.

Wade inland next, through seaweed,
clamber up a shell mound,
thread thickets of thorn with
long pants and sleeves dripping,
our faces and hands
speckled with mosquitoes.

Once on the island, uninhabited now
after hurricane storm surges left only
chards from native peoples
and bricks from later folks, we sense
mingled ghosts from centuries.

We grin now not to mind
heat, nor how we look,
barely civilized, torn,

alive from salt tides,

wide skies, bites and burns

giving blood, giving homage,

on this day joined with

ancient selves

in all beauty and water.

Speechless

Four sandhill cranes make their
unhurried stroll into my yard.

They could fly, but they walk,
heads up, elegant.

The younger two may
waver from a straight path to
dawdle and try the sand for a bug.

With a scoop of millet seed in hand,
I open the door, it creaks,
and they all pretend alarm.
Gray feathers flutter,
skinny legs give a hop.

So I walk carefully, slowly, at their speed,
as they take a few steps back, and
I spread the yellow millet they prefer.
Then sitting on the porch, I watch them
pick and peck at the strewn gold.
I like to imagine a low burble of thanks.

Later, in the evening,
I hear them across the lake,
their full-throated bugling.

Big Island Ballet

in the blue light
the turtle glides down
legs outstretched like wings
graceful through a watery forest
of sun rays

a school of green fish flicks florescent tails all
at the same moment

swimming with fins and snorkel
I see the tapestry back of the turtle
medieval echoes perhaps from its past life
the fibonacci numbering of its plates from god
who often loves mathematical order

what is on my back I wonder and who is looking
at it as I move along

I feel naked here not
knowing my part finding myself on this
perfect stage
where everything seems art
seems choreographed

so I try to appear graceful
act cool as though this water world
is my natural element nodding my head
this way and that fish-like taking it all in as though
it were an ordinary morning a usual thing
to find myself in such celestial company

the turtle moves travels with me for a minute
and the green fish too as we follow a white
sand path between tall aquatic weeds

then at the opening of a larger pool
we separate with flips of fins gliding again
to our many lives

Ichetucknee Canoe

We're floating downstream
not paddling.
Moving alongside us, a clump
of water lettuce.
We don't talk.
We glide and slide,
green water, blue water,
bright plants.

Reflections ripple
over gray-white tree trunks,
over our skin and
the sides of canoes,
the legs of herons,
the feathers and face of
the still owl
peering at us.

We are clothed alike –
a team, a family,
all shining
in this river's one light.

Lake Morning

After a sunrise extravaganza
the lake rests from visibility,
a white cloud hour
until the midmorning warmth
pushes off fog and curls water
into waves of sky-reflecting blue.

I, too, enjoy a quiet time before
I invite the breeze to ripple my brain waves,
hoping to be as wide ranging
as the wind, at least for a while, letting me
play free across borders, drop enmity,
offer me to light.

Brook Farms

Death throes of a star
make gold

        star-shaped leaves
        unfold

        pines' yellow candles
glow

sounds of births, moaning
breaking open boulders, ice

        rivers, lovers
        dragonflies and bulrushes,
        gardens and calluses

listen to the brushes
        of the artists

A New Sunflower Species

The planet rolls,
the sun sends banners across
the yard as expected, but this morning
unexpected blooms about two feet across
erupt, flowers of light that seem
alive.

Cavern

Over a fence, a trespass across a field,
an unmarked cave entrance, a careful clamber.
Friends went down first, I followed.
Once inside, bones of a fox, scat of a bat, cool relief,
quiet chamber, room enough for a Neanderthal family,
for runaways from war or slavery,
for a bear, or a bank-robbing gang escaping the law.
Emptiness where imagination can play, a mind expand.

In one dark passage I asked them to leave me behind.
Be along in a sec. Their flashlights dimmed,
their voices disappeared; I pushed further in.

I am deep in the earth now.
I have been here before. This narrow channel,
somehow comfortable,
a longed-for home. I sit on a ledge,
rest my feet on an opposite wall,
welcome in an ancient temple of dark and stillness.

Greens of August

On a certain day in August,
the greens will battle blues,
stars and folks will line up
for colors they will choose.

Ginger cones stay moist
as greens begin to thirst.
Vines will leap their highest
just as their seed pods burst.

All know the outcome,
and still the effort soars.
Greens will outdo summer with
fall's fireworks, of course.

I See You, But So What

That squirrel knew how long it would take me
to leave the window and open the door,
so it had no need to hurry off,
in fact, plenty of time
to pull out a few more mouthfuls
from where it had eaten through the bottom
of the bag I'd left there thinking it was safe.
The squirrel's math had mine beat,
rewarding it with a buffet of bird seed.

Yeah baby, that squirrel was relaxed, laid back
in a hammock of bent space-time.

Today's Tropical Adrenaline

I am on the porch, horizontal rain hitting me.
A bird feeder blows over. Sound
sizzles. I'm in an audio of a boiling pot.

A slash of light.

I'm dodging death in
a fast-forward movie of my life.

No beams or bones crack. My movie screen
doesn't go black. A few palm fronds torn to the ground.
The hummingbirds come back out
and head for a stiff drink.

Old Women and the Weeds

You could eat the spiderwort flower,
but please don't.
Consider the beauty of it
sturdy in disturbed soil,
fumes or fresh air,
unkempt yard or highway side.

The busy bouncing squirrel
scallops across the yard,
doesn't stop to sniff or
take in the indigo or amethyst of it,
but you and I, moving slowly,
we do.

Vultures and Winter Rye

On sandy ground where little grows,
where a bouquet of nettle or
a lump of red-tipped moss are treasures, a patch
of rye flares bright green. This fragile grass
burns brown at first summer sun, lives here now
to surprise the winter.

These wet, thin blades
hold the impression of a footfall for hours.
If only it were tough
so I could roll in it and live on it,
but I skirt it carefully,
water it, walk around it.
Such color!

Look – turkey vultures overhead!
I like vultures. They don't kill,
they clean the world of rotting carcasses.
We owe them gratitude.
Do they see a new landmark from the sky?
Are they, like me, a glad audience
to this aberrant spot of joy, this elfin lawn
beside the cabin in the woods?

Freeze Forecast in a Blue Moon

Good moonlight,
so tucking sheets
around the giant
philodendron tonight
was easy.
I had a big pocket
full of clothespins.
It took five queen-size
sheets. When I stood
back, pleased, I saw
the philodendron had become
a second moon, gracing
my yard, perfectly
round, white, glowing.

Winter Dawn

When the ground is January brown
when kids grab orange crayons
and rub themselves for warmth
when clouds hang in the kitchen
when the saucepan steams
and the family breath is solid
when the oven door's
left open and the windows steam up
when the newspaper leaves
a patch of dry ground underneath
when tennis shoes never dry
when sand sticks to wet dog feet
when dawn is a cold wound
for mercurochrome sun
when the bare red coils of stove and toaster
threaten and comfort
when fires scare and caress
when noses and chimneys smoke
and lake mists shift and rise
as winds whistle out of earth's teakettle
give thanks when sun makes winter trees and frost
glow orange, give thanks for winter fields
blooming with pink and golden light

Ravine Ritual

On the ridge, stare canopy birds in the eye
ease down into the crevasse,
pause there by the stream,
where earth warbles its alive call.

If you see three deer, burble clear water sounds.
They will hold still, think you curious and harmless,
more amused than convinced
by your creek imitation.

Look up from the ravine
through the stars of the sweet gum leaves
look high where spring green meets blue sky,
refuse any words but prayer.

Begin the steep return, grateful for gravity's dancing
lessons, the deep breaths, push and pull, lift and dip,
descent, and climb, laugh
to be able to dance both parts.

Ripening

let dancers dance, let all

talents aching for outlet

find them

let raking combs find

fleas in the cat fur

let bitter cold beads of water vapor

find the cores they need

bacterium or micrometeorite

aloft from home planets

making possible the raindrop and snowflake

yes let neglected hard knobs of wild pears

become an uproar of rejoicing

as crows sing out each drooling beak full

Yellow Fly Season

Flying in on gold wings to
dig their stingers in skin,
they go for blood.

The hound, with no escape,
lies immobilized
in tortuous itch, perhaps

winning transcendence
like the Yanomamo who calmly
endure insect bites.

Painting a house, I finally
give up on repellants
and slaps, let

be my bare legs,
yellow flies pinned to
my flesh like jewels.

The hound discovers refuge
under the house all day,
coming out only to greet

our return as she exposes
herself to flights of
poison-tipped darts. Flies

cover her bloodied nose, take
advantage of her distraction,
her fond heart.

Three Generations Clearing Weeds from the Lake

The middle guy makes the deals,
carries the business cards,
calls me and texts, drinks coffee.

The big old guy is the dad whose
bulk can tolerate the cold best, so he rakes
sitting in a chair in chest-high water.

The young guy, thin,
doesn't say hello to me,
brings himself sodas, power drinks.

The middle guy wades near the shore,
muscles burning but
barreling through, roaring orders.

Then precarious and upright in the sliding boat,
he pulls up deep grasses with his long rake,
a ballet of balance, shoulders shining.

The old guy probably appreciates
the support of the water, tugs
hard-to-pull weeds. He waves, friendly.

The young guy drives the tractor, boom box booming,
with a pitchfork heaves heavy green piles
onto the trailer, unloads them at the edge of the woods.

The middle guy pockets the cash
saying he works for fear of the Lord,
not just the money.

The Lord seems to like
the three hard-working guys
opening the lake to the sky.

Cold Snap

The last day of winter today,
yet last night the first hard freeze

I think the birds were
shocked by it---a portent—they

had stuffed themselves at the feeder,
had emptied it overnight, so

this morning I wrapped myself in coat and
scarf against the sharp wind,

filled the feeders,
chuckling and grumbling

at the rosy breasted finches
I suspected were overhead watching,

"Hungry ones, you thought
an icy doom had come,"

As though I didn't understand
the need to fatten when famine

seems to loom, I looked up to the birds
for an all's well,

and my searching eyes found a yes in
the piercing blue of the sky, our home.

Squash Blossom Summer

Untitled

driving alone
on the night-quiet street
romance of neon
kissing dark
like fireflies

running away
from touches
saying no to desire
to images beckoning
in oak branches
shapes in moon shades
the almost
so close

Food of an Affair

So new was our talk and touch,
we abandoned full-scale meals.
Brief bits of food that became
our custom, I remember still.

The blueberries under the white
avalanche of yogurt, wheat bread,
butter and honey, as we lay awake until dawn.

A ceremony, the gelled and jeweled gold
of a pineapple wedge eaten under
the umbrella of bright green catalpa
and the foam of its white blossoms.

The shape of the lime-drenched avocado
echoed the shapes of our breasts
cradled in each other's hands.

The artichoke we shared with rapt
attention, moving leaf by leaf
into the thin-veiled, transparent
lavender petals at the center,
held up then, for the moon to shine through.

Our tongues took the juice of the wild

grape, avoiding its bitter seed.

Careful, we spoke of an unadorned present,

of beauty and not of love.

Kentucky Bourbon

In the bottom land mud took its time

to dry

and boys took their time

to speak

weather spoke for us and clouds dropped

lines

girls' shirts implied

touch

first breasts, first cigarette, first car,

first fuck,

first duck kill, first chew

mud sucked us into its clutches

first planting

Platonic

Not reaching for each other's skin,
we meet in the air.
This kind of affair,
we dance forward in the mind, curtsy,
step back, it's that simple.

It's not that simple airily caring.
Cactus spines of restraint
pine to loosen,
discard themselves, leave pure pulp,
unhurried, smooth, sturdily plump.

Forbidden, such an old-fashioned word.
Not bidden, this passion
stirred and hidden,
a country dance of
austere Jane Austen, yet
when hummingbirds come home
and cranes have flown,
even blown-by-the-wind
seeds may take root some
squash blossom summer.

Kissing Cousins

In West Virginia, they called them kissing cousins,
those who married each other, and we laughed
at those, while we kissed our own
cousins and needed no definitions since those kisses
took place in secret, often in a tent created by a sheet,
when lights were out and eyes were closed
and no words uttered. Where else
was one to find the ways of love
but with cousins, and ways to bathe
each other but never come clean, never tell?

It seemed almost okay somehow,
priestly elder cousins absolving all wrong.
No discussion, no questions,
and knowledge flooded in easily.

Secrets were taped to the back of the mind's drawers,
drawers quite functional, holding bras, socks, and jewelry.
Coded confessions might never be found, and the
slight adrenaline moisture in the palm, well,
the southern summer fan will take care of that.
Since cousins look alike, thought we were in the same family,
even kind of owned each other, we never owned up
to any should-not, ought-not.
It was a fiction, like a dream, like a movie, the reality

of it passed when the lights went on. Only popcorn on the
skirt, popcorn kernels in the bra left traces.

In the kitchen mornings after our mischief
we were experts in denial,
pouring out cereal with no regrets.
Nor was there need to say *I'm sorry* or *Don't tell* or
*I was in a fog, I was asleep, I'm going
to marry soon*. Did we remember touches,
kneading the bag of white margarine until the
orange color-ball popped and spread throughout,
until it looked and tasted yellow, just as it should.
Did memory testify *When my cousin touched a breast,
heat spread over my body until I knew
what my body could be, and I wanted it to
taste bright and gold and shining in the sun.*

Body Surfing

The years when we make love,
sex comes like a perfect wave,
this is it, get on, take it in
foam over our backs
heads burrowed in a sea rush
minds left behind
in yesterday's sunlight. We become
dolphins arcing up and down,
no bones, all curves,
no words, all sounds.

But when we don't make love,
the wave doesn't come,
we push off and float, arms ready
to throw forward.
But the wave won't break –
it will point up and
lift us off our feet and
set us back down again,
still in our right minds. The top
won't turn over and explode us
across the surface, the words
remain words. They don't dissolve
into seagull cries.

No, sky doesn't divide the sea

to turn the world inside out.

Its wide reach holds us and

in our open-eyed good day,

it's still hard to leave the water,

to leave this calm ocean now,

this quiet place the wild and perfect waves

brought us to a while ago.

Couple Seeks Geographical Cure

Fog on the west coast for the first day, sheltering
exposed tidepools with moist, cool air
soothing nerves exposed by arguing and
caffeine, a long day on an airplane.

Travel gambles – shuffles two sides
of a pack of cards – chance
and planning – luck
and skill. This coast, that coast.
What will it be? Will we fall in love again?

It seems to be working, we are
holding closer to each other than usual,
with strangeness all around us,
and ourselves somehow strange, too.

September Bardo

I am floundering in the bardo
between lives
with a partner or alone.

Dead branches fall from the water oak,
a sign of rot in the trunk.
In imagination I see the heavy tree tilt
and crash on my bedroom, taking down roof
and security, letting in torrents and raccoons
and rats.

Hard to make the decision to cut it down,
to lose its shade, its dangerous grandeur.

Zombie Love

You said you were alive.
I believed you, I even
defended you to friends
who said you were so
transparent, they could
see through you. Too much
screen time makes lives,
eyes bleary, out of touch,
not requiring reality
or remembering it. My
fingers made speech.
I could hear the words
of your letters. But didn't
a smell rise over the keys?
Didn't a cloud of moisture
cover the screen and drip
on the desk? Didn't the image bulge
and shrink, the eyes open,
finally slide into a puddle
vapidly evaporating,
known finally as barely there,
gone, as nothing.

'Bye Sug

You don't mean
to be treacherous;

Something in my chemistry
turns your
sweetness sour, so

go on to others
with skill to take
you in.

I'll take up the
challenge of
letting you go.

I'll sink in to the
couch, the bed, the day
without you,

shudder
and rest.

Sincerely,
Me

Divorce

Divorce was very quiet,
the world was still asleep,
coffee, orange juice on the run
no time to stay and weep.

It tiptoed through the house
slowly closed the door,
left the key under the mat
not needed anymore.

It didn't say its name out loud
to sky or forest floor
nor had to take the photos down
that never hung before.

How very smooth, how current,
no tiresome knot untied.
Kismet's kiss took blame for
divorce's slow landslide.

Sailor's Farewell

I'm not the north to your compass
however determined I was,
hollering from the south, for
equatorial warmth of equity, but
my calls failed, seemed
more distraction than attraction,
more magma than magnet.

So I'm hardening to lava rock,
an island in the sea with
great purples and magentas,
alizarins and lizards, wallop of
whale tail, dawns running long into day,
sunsets longing deep into night.

Sticking Points

How soon it began:
You hung out of a window
to jokingly throw an insult.
See ya later, jerk!

I should have quit then.
You should have quit then.
Thousands of wondrous times
interlaced with thousands
of name-callings and
we were still glued together.

I knew you would edit me.
Every sentence was faulty,
every evening had its fight.
Turn off the light!
You should have, you shouldn't have.
Why didn't you, why did you.
Jerk became *child*, became *idiot*.

Memories never synched.
You said *No, I didn't.*
I said *No you didn't.*
The ocean roar gave us privacy
to argue in public. *The surf is too rough,*

*don't go in. Don't be a wimp. Pick up your
feet. Don't eat that.
I need to sleep. It's too early.*

Boxing ring won over
the wedding ring.
We couldn't marry,
we couldn't divorce.

Yet after years of not kissing, we could
sleep close in a guest bed, as easy
as in the early years. I can still cry
remembering the hard love we had.

Not Medusa

Her head grew locks,
locks hanging, clanging
against each other,
against her, against me.

Sometimes now, I come across
a rusty key.
Ah, should I go
back, should I
try again?

Midsummer Night's Eve

When I look at everything
frightening and unlovely
in her and can still
say *yes, why not*
even though the why nots
mount up to a tall list.

Lightning strikes beside
the car. I can feel it
in my teeth. I can
see its branches of fire,
bright and loud,
two strikes in one spot,
a tower of a hundred
fires like my
tower of why nots
burning.

On the Verge

Driving alone
on the quiet night street
trying not to see romance
in the neon-kissing dark
running away from touches
saying no to desire
to images of hands
beckoning in oak branches
to shapes of lovers in moon shadows,
the almost
so close.

After Mallarmé

My love sits tranquil this morning,
after the autumn storm had stripped
the blooms from her roses.
Now I rake up,
disrupt a toad seeking shelter.
My heart, I don't mean to be cruel.
Give him a home, ma cherie,
and she guides me to set a cracked pot
under the oak for a toad's winter home.
Beside it, a turquoise saucer of water
holds the sky for the toad and us.
From a certain angle
my love sees reflected
the rose petal that flew and
attached to her hair.

Breakup in November

Under the leafless branches
of pecan trees, I watch you
and the road wave up and down
like a shook blanket.

The pecans' green hulls have split to
release the nuts to the ground and
we have tossed them rattling
into hollow metal buckets.

Goodbye to the blisses
and hissing crickets,
of hot firefly nights,
passion season, passed.

Running, ripping off clothes
I thrash out a bitter swim,
throw my body stinging with icy cold
on the warm sand beach.

On the inside of my eyelids,
alternating sunlight and shadows
make amazing moire patterns,
the dazzle, the dance.

I laugh in goofy ecstasy after pain,

fuck you, bless you.

I can find the water here,

I can find the well.

These Days with Us

Just as our bodies curl around
each other and seek each other
out in endless interest,
our thoughts receive
new angles and delight
in returning words spun with
fresh energy. Our world
is smiling with us these days
and we pray, giving
thanks. May all refugees
find such homes.

In Love Again

Sago palm, you
fecund bulb,

perfection of math and art and ease,
visible Fibonacci spiraling
blessings.

Goddess!
Hadron Collider
has nothing on you,

central particle, plan,
holding it all together
clearly evident.

I can feel it in
my chest, Higgs Boson
in the bosom
best evidence.

I am here to
convince everyone everywhere,
I am here to testify.

Poem for Pat

Over the top is the only way
to reflect the world, we agreed,
admiring Pat's new mirror
circled with 39 little mirrors of our faces.

Look at Pat's windows shine,
even the oak leaves outside
sparkle like polished silver.

Feel the heart leap at the sight of friends
our inexplicable harmonizing.

No way to exaggerate
describing this stuff, what we are,
and what's all around us,
branching, leafing.

The cat is wary of our excitement
but stays with us.

A day to live,
a day to plant, a day to prune,
a day to sing.

Lovers turn into ex-lovers then
into friends, and friends
turn to life-long loves.

Cups turn from half-empty
to half-full, from half-full
to spilling over.

Saucerie

"No," you stopped me. "Don't wash the pan.
Pour off the grease, all but a spoonful,
scrape the gristly scraps loose, add herbs, a little wine
or coconut milk, you'll have a fine sauce.

"At the bottom of every pan is a harbor
of possibility. Select notes will float like
buoys to signal the deep channel,
places where river water

and saltwater meet. Osmotic release of energy,
an elixir. The remains will sing like a choir."
Who knew? I didn't even know you could cook.
"Enjoy," you say, "enjoy!"

Haiku

Growling, she was, rough
as an oyster shell, still, I
wanted the oyster.

Sago and Spirals

The Point of Palms

leaves incisive

crisp sound and shadow

trunk decisive visible

geometric triangles neatly

arranged order

Fibonacci fives and eights

sago palm presents tada!

perfect sculpture

of double spirals

every year

clipped beats

to dance to

the world isn't mush, they say

we are not and you are not

while your body is alive while

you're here in it

there's a counting

and a rhythm thing

going on

Solstice and the Changing Seen

Waves seen at eye level,
how is it there's
a dark side
and a bright at once?

Or are they alternating,
like separation anxiety
that both clings and
tries to let go?

At solstice the sun
stands still between
shortening and
lengthening light.

At the water surface,
rain leaps up into
pearls, floating,
perfect for a moment.

The observer changes,
the view changes, and then
it all disappears, like
prayers in the air.

Five of my friends died this year.

Two, last week. In my heart,

love and grief

wrestle to a draw.

Triptych

On the black bull with curved horns
a pudgy little man sits cross-legged,
Control of passions, my father said.

A girl and boy take turns
somersaulting over
bulls, placing hands on the back
flipping between the horns.
Playing with danger, my mom said.

Another voice calls,
Come here, says Selene,
the bull-horned moon goddess,
I open my crescent arms to you.

Life on a Pedestal

Something backwards here. Being
hammered and split and chipped.
In whose courtyard must I
hold a fountain? In what gallery
will my eyes be wide-open all night?
In this studio, who will sweep up
my particles, dusty and sharp?

Art After

The page shone so white
she took to it with a pen
like a snow shovel

each swing of her arm
lifting a mass of snow
leaving a black line that

others could follow into
a lost archive
a trail where hounds might

sniff in the cold to say
someone was here
there was life under the ice

at least a memory
of deep-fried beignet
and trombone

she traced this narrow path
'til she found a hot spring
steaming on the cold page

Anne Sexton Dream

I dreamed Anne Sexton clerked a store where
I was looking for shoes.   *How about these?*
You have nice toes, show them off, she said,
in fact you have nice arches.   She took
my foot in her hand.   You write books, I said,
awestruck. *Did I?* Yes.   Would you autograph
my ankle like a bracelet?   Would it seem too
girly? *Not at all.   I once fell in love with a*
therapist.   Now I am a therapist.   I write so
to speak, on feet.   I find a Cinderella,
and I play the prince of course, a beautiful prince.
I heal.   Please don't say it.
No sex or heel puns and no Sylvia Plath references,
none of her fascist feet.   Just let me be tender
with your foot.   We'll be a poem together,
live again, get things right.

My One and Only Poem to Charles Bukowski

OMG I am reading
Charles Bukowski,
he's getting a cancer
burnt out of his
nose, cauterized, the doc
sends him home
in shock.
You said it, Charles,
you laid it out like
a poker hand.
I blink.
OMG I have the same
sore in my nose.
Me and Charles Bukowski!
Our noses twitching
in the same way, both
our fingers exploring
our same little
anomaly.

Valentine to a Poet

After I am in your presence,
I look different in the mirror. Turn,
lift eyebrows, unbutton at neck,
roll sleeves.

I can see someone new
in those eyes, someone
not me. How do
you do it?

With a key, a push,
an invitation. You do it
slapping words on the table,
daring me.

Rash Diagnosis and Diogenes's Lamp

It spreads, the red on my flesh,
like a very pale blush, starts on my
cheeks, at first, I look rosy-faced, out
of breath, but *exhilarated* becomes *puffy-faced*.
My shoulders then, had I used the wrong soap
at the hotel? Hotel! Was it bedbugs?
The rash spreads in my mind,
prickles start on my back. No good mirror.
Would someone look? Would someone put
lotion on? Or would no one want to touch?
Am I spreading it when I shower? Would hot
water be bad, ice water be nice?
The new laundry soap
said *antiallergenic* but is it new enough?
My breasts now, my stomach. Is it the polyester sheets?
The air handler, the bonfire next door?
In my dreams, I go to a new job and I'm late
the first day, unprepared to teach and nude,
wearing only rash.
Is it just winter, the dry air,
the winter wool clothes, the long underwear,
the cat hair in the couch, the fiberglass in the filter?
Was it Borax in the kitchen, some wire burning,
should I apply aloe or take herbs or is the laptop
sending vapors? Did I wash the apples and lettuce

enough, did I touch the Christmas tree, did I touch

a public toilet, a doorknob, should I stay home

or stay out of my home? Should I use exfoliant or

loofa or avoid them? Are there squirrels

in the walls or squirrelly ideations?

Is it the beginning of decline, the last days arriving?

I Want to Be Worthy: A Sermon for Self

What a vain yearning. Does the breeze ask that of me?
It tickles my legs, my arms, the leaves on my trees.
The breeze doesn't care if I'm a scoundrel,
leaves sparkle, happy being themselves.

I let go my heavy spirit, levitate,
look to support environmentalists
protecting the planet that gives us so much,
giving back to the trees, water, air.

That warrior working against the oil
pipeline, may need some water, a sandwich.
That weary door to door canvasser might want to dance,
I am being given, so I hope to give myself.

When the moon goddess was to visit, the rabbit worried.
*What have I to offer? The fox is beautiful, the monkey
is clever,
I am neither.* So the rabbit threw herself on the campfire.

Here I am, I am all I have and I give you my all.

And the goddess snatched up the rabbit.
Come here into my arms, rabbit.
Will you come to the moon with me?

And now we see

the rabbit with the moon goddess,

smiling down at us,

though we may not know our worth.

Time, You're a Rowdy Hag Like Me

Time, you slippery freak, I can't
get my footing. Sliding
on my butt into July, I
grab for a perfect ice axe reverse.
Well, iced coffee reverse.

Time, you're a rowboat I
can't leap from onto shore
without that equal and opposite
shove that pushes the boat back and
dumps me flat on the shallow
with twisted ankle, swallowing water and muck.

Time, at least there's adrenaline
in your cheap rush, as I go skating
in my socks across your polished floor,
alarming my neighbor. *It's okay,*
I scream, *Whee! I'll leave the house to you!*

Beware All-Consuming Passions

Purple blotches on the bare face,

bare-faced lie about being hit,

blush to be caught wearing blush --

this is the song of a woman who loves too long.

This is the rhythm of a woman who dreams

Here is the politic of paucity,

shimmering shame of coins in the fountain,

desire desperate and ordinary,

necklace chains that leave stain like a noose.

Never enough rings the till.

Vespers

When cranes bugle for an evening bite, it's time
to scatter seeds, and for our table
gather a handful of lyre leaf sage.
Sunset will give us a chance to breathe, then

take in the war news,
slick video soundbytes
we think we must know.
No bugler sounds a charge,

showers of shrapnel carve flesh from
bones, cranes fly off like transmigration
to the next life.
Jeopardy comes after the news.

Sleep Tight

She smooths sheets and covers,
looks at the half glass of water, the teeth sunk in it.
"Do we need more water?"
This standing person touches and tucks in
the person in bed.

"We're not going to drink out of that glass now,
with our teeth in it, are we?" She laughs at her joke.
"Do we need another blanket,
the bathroom light on, the door open
so you can see out?"

So you can see in.

"Why are you
kicking under the covers?

My legs are held down by the blanket.
She shovels dirt over me and says

"Goodnight, dear, sleep tight."

One Shoe

Waiting for the other shoe to drop isn't a strategy
for accepting the inevitable. Waiting is arbitrary,
not the only way. Life isn't a toaster about to pop, a
teakettle about to scream, a bill sure to be in the mail.

Life isn't tomorrow's wrinkles, isn't having to
move out of the house, a limited usage plan.
Life isn't about dying, it flat out is not death.
Predictions are only forecast, aperitif, mere teasing.

Those with hands cupped to the ears, those
in the lower apartments, under the first shoe,
under the buoyant bed springs, are waiting in vain,
effects waiting for causes, psychic suicide at best.

Merlin, the guy who aged backwards, is a fairy tale.
Don't wait for the other shoe to drop. It's the present
moment that will feed us, and never,
blessedly, in the way we expect.

The Journals of Lost Brothers

The man said he heard his brother crying for help.
A sinkhole had opened under him, pulling him, his bed,
his walls down to a cavern, and over him, rocks and
dirt piled. His sister was left with a torn bible.
"The Lord gave us a message."

My own brother left journals of voices
and hallucinations. "I may be dying," he wrote
in his last words, "but I'm in God's hands."

Another brother was struck forever
speechless by lightning. The stuff of myth,
earth opening up, swallowing like a gullet, and lightning
like a brainstorm, a bolt of insight: weather the storm.

Tell that to the
fat earth, tell that to the dry cold wind,
tell that to the stuttering tongue and the burnt
hair. Tell that to the sky.

Holy Day USA

I know how to pray to do my part
to prepare for a holy day. I will
dilate eyes so fishes jump higher
with bigger long-lasting splashes,

I will hear more voices as music.
When the calendar
closes its eyes on a year, I will bow
and close my eyes too.

I will make way for change, let some hills level,
lose a tree, know my dear road
will go new places, look unfamiliar, I may forgive,
may break bread with a grudge.

Oedipus may open his eyes and see
father and mother marry in
passionate innocence. Like spring rain
apologies may ease down on the grasses and families.

The underwear of anger
may disintegrate in harp notes.
The darling child on the horizon
will walk barefoot on soft mosses.

Pi Day

From afternoon alive with bugs,
mists enumerate with dew,
the shining pines stand coyly
attracting goldfinch crew.

Splash, you bass of splendid swim,
tease you troll from creaking bridge.
Day will happen without a vote,
blisses, without a stitch.

Silver Delicious

Hard to tell tastes from images in this downpour.
Night, tart and wet as an apple,
offers rain emoting with pitch changes,
volume changes, a choir.

No more the obsessively taunting voices from
my childhood. Off you went, demons,
to wherever you go. Now,
shake it loose, say the Shakers. *Have an apple*,
says Eve. Our new place uncluttered, for
dance and cider, like a church with no pews, has
space to twirl and fall.

Rain whispers, *Have a bite, it's good.*

Aging with You

Over breakfast we talk
about aging, the clichés
of cream of wheat or dishes of prunes
are set aside, and bibs are still resisted.

Finger joints freeze, harder to make
a G seventh or C seventh chord.
Loose skin drapes over muscles
as strong as ever because
going to the gym has become church.

We avoid speaking of who might die first,
though obituary scanning
supersedes new clothing ads.
Our eyes look fascinated at veins,
at each other's wrinkles.

Hands reach for the partner's hands,
so in love, so grateful.

Vernal Equinox

Once again day equals night,
once again there's time for

being outside with the blotches
and bruises, axes, chain saw.

We dismantle a fence.
You muscled it, my friend said.

I think she saw my recklessness,
heedless of snakes, nails,

pulling post and wire loose,
hacking through smilax thorns,

ardisia and spider webs,
pruning amongst the briars to let

the blossoming wild plum tree
have space. It all rolls around,

comes back, the moment when
the vine caught my foot and

and I knew I was falling. I still
wear signs of where I've been,

the look of someone returning,
of having once lost my balance.

Twelve

Midnight, the gift

of the weird godmother

the pumpkin hour, first watch of the night.

The black

sinkhole of day, the most irony

of any hour. Crazed

clouds pass over the moon

clang twelve,

kill and bring to life

today's last chance, tomorrow's first,

moment between breaths, between lives,

when nothing is known

moment of readiness, ugly moment

that wants revenge, moment that prays or

preys upon itself,

a moment that breaks windows, tears off doors,

a moment exploding with winged seeds.

Take a new name at the pumpkin hour.

You are not the person you were.

Break Out

will it be ice in the river fracturing in spring

will it be a relationship ripped apart

will it be a break-in and loss of a Martin guitar and

Granny's necklace

will tears pour out of a red face

will the blocked artist release a new kind of painting

when a friend dies, will I remember to be grateful to have

lived with love

will I remember that love is the other side of grief

will I remember to break out singing

to break out dancing

will I roar and wail

I want to take a big break from the silly imperative

of the ceaseless smile,

crack open, get hatched

Keeping Up Appearances

Be sure to put cream on your elbows.
Be sure to shave before work.

Remember to compost, remember
to take cloth bags to the grocery.
Be sure to count the sodium milligrams,
read the labels, nitrates, sulfites.

Keep an appointment book;
remember your brother's birthday.
Say hi to those that don't want you to drink.
Look them in the eye.

They think they don't want
to be around the stupid acting folks;
I think they don't want to feel tempted,
they envy me getting the edge off,
feeling too on edge themselves,
hoped I would be a mainstay of strength for them
instead find me drinking. Meanwhile

be sure to keep some pencils,
sharpened ones with good erasers,
to hug more, to take movies and books
back to the library even when

you haven't finished them,

and in the morning, practice recalling

what you can of the night before.

Palaces of the Poor

The columns only imitated a plantation,
made of tin, not horsehair, sand, and molasses.
Still, for a few years it was their palace,
a mansion with echoes of old wealth,
vast rooms with sparse furniture.

One of her chores was to tend the furnace, fetch coal,
another to keep the porch swept, repeat, repeat,
soporifics giving time for daydreaming,
a new battle jacket to cheer in, plays to write,
snubs to consider and try to toss aside.

At night under those lofty columns she watched
the wobble of moons between the maples
as she struggled, nauseated, determined
to learn to smoke, two puffs enough
to make it difficult to stand.

She managed to get to college,
to quit smoking, to be a competition diver
with a strong sense of the vertical,
get steady, have ambitions for her children,
teach literature for decades.

Seventy years later in an Alzheimer's unit,
she will hallucinate that house, live in it again,
turn it into a clinic. She will say of a doctor,
walking through the hospital room she thinks
is her old bedroom, *That's Polonius.*

Her brain will tangle
like the metallic clinkers she retrieved
from under the coals.
Where are you, Hamlet? Where is Horatio?
she will ask a nurse.

She will endure
a drawn-out, messed-up ending,
though she wanted an almost suicide,
a perfect dive, with no over-rotation,
an impeccable entry into death.

How to Tell if You're a Poet

When you're a poet
    you eat oranges you say oranges
        you spend a lot of money on
socks, get the rest of your clothes cheap, you
hoe in a garden and leave
    weeds in your lawn.
Clouds tell you
     things. You gather
  words like acorns. Squirrels and cranes are your
cousins, all children your children.

You might look into the future
    you might not, you might do
       a ritual you might not.
You will love tea
    and, of course, the moon, whose
       phases and whereabouts you track.
Even in the dark of the moon,
    you know where it's gone, you
       hear what that moon is saying.

Travel Tales

Drought At Goldhead

She could hardly speak of it — where
the lake had been was now
a flattened bowl of charred brown,
a color she had never seen in nature.
She noticed how people said, "Have you been down
to the lake?" as though

a decorous word like *deceased*
hadn't been thought of yet for gone lakes.
She watched people still walking
the old shore path, looking out
where a few black branches lay exposed,
preserved like wrecks from old storms.

Finally, she waded into the
chill of invisible waters
to stare mesmerized at
patterns of cracked mud,
careful as cobblestones, long
crooked fissures of longing, lament.

Solo Roads and the Single Girl

The slush on the tire wheel made a starburst.
I saw it traveling cross-country once
as a sign of the rightness of the universe, so reckless
I took acid and drank and watched a tv without images
and lay down naked in the snow outside the motel door
and got too friendly with a stranger. I put him off
by promising to meet the next day
 and told my girlfriend in the morning
we've got to get out of here early. We never told anyone
we were together.

Later in my sober drugless years, I traveled alone
with remnants of a drinking urge and a flu,
and when I was lonely, I went to AA. Pretty tough,
sitting in a small room with the smokers,
but I had no one else to talk to, no one
else to listen to. After AA, I went to a psychic
fair, which led to a visit with UFO
watchers whose appeal to me was they
welcomed me as well as aliens. They believed love
could bring peace to all. Worth a try.

I ran into other loners. On a scenic path by the ocean
a homeless man found a bush to sleep under. That's
travel. Not in the same town, same house all the time.

Not enough time to get jaded, not enough time
to get pinched by the stays. I learned about
corset stays from my grandmother
who never traveled once she moved
to Evansville, Indiana. She and her clothes stayed put.
She didn't even let grandfather see her naked.

Travel sheds costumes and customs,
doles out delicious moods
and delusions.
I see a sign I may be breaking
up with my current girlfriend and I will go
traveling, a blue highway thing,
following a wandering star.

Ode to Heat

A feather pillow to relax into,
the humming fans and creaking porch swings of old
we've still got, the marimba music of ice cubes in glasses,
the swimming in the wonder of Florida's cold springs.
A lot of heat, though, you just
want to send to Alaska.

Some summers will heat a coin on a patio table so hot
you can't hold it long enough to get it to a cold drink
machine. You know that kind of heat?

When you set an apple on the dashboard
and it bakes before you get to a corner
and after you've turned a couple of corners
the apple rolls from side to side and makes applesauce.

When the cafeteria cooks are missing from the kitchen
because they're hanging out in the walk-in cooler.
When you pray that the other fat person comes to
meditation group so they'll turn on the air conditioning,
and tai chi seems too vigorous.

When your new haircut disappears
as soon as your head starts sweating,
which happens at the register as you're paying.

It's hot when the molecules move faster
and the people move slower,
and we eat less and drink more, and when we do eat,
we eat potato chips for the salt; you know heat
is a great excuse for potato chips.

Heat's a challenge to creativity.
I know a hot femme who keeps her
underwear in the freezer
for the delicious cool moment of slipping into
those chilly panties.

Great sex is called hot sex, and romance heats up.
It limbers us up like it does arthritis, it makes us mellow
and willing to sit in one place for a long time.
A hot passion can last like a truly hot fire
and the coals can last even longer.

Heat has the same letters as hate, but it's more ambivalent,
more like love . . . sometimes you move toward it,
sometimes away from it.
And heat is like coffee and love,
with regard to temperature, there's a precise line below
which neither coffee nor love is worth pursuing
and above which both are dangerous.

Like when you're driving to Hot-lanta
and you hang magazines over your left arm
and left knee to protect
them from sun blazing through the window,

and you get drowsy on the highway and look for
a patch of shade, a sweet green glade
where you can pull over and take a nap,
but it can be the deadly road
versus the deadly rest stop
and you'd better make that nap quick
or the shade will move,
and in that conversation,
heat will have the last word.

Poet at an Outdoor Restaurant

Opening the paper's bad
news, she heads for the crossword
that seems a kind word.

Now the breathtaking sunset,
just a brief glitter of coin
dropping through smoke and haze
into the piggybank of Best Buy,
worth watching across four lanes.

A Pilgrimage to See Sister Maggie

High in the night sky, clouds seem
to break into tufts almost too light
to fly. Snow is a miracle
to a Floridian. I watch awed
as frost stars sigh around with
no direct drop to the ground, no
hurry to become hardened icing
under foot. They blow sideways, often
preferring perches on heads and noses
of statues who accept them
without resistance or sneezing.

They're statues after all, of the holy family,
standing near the entrance to the convent.
and I'm the initiate pagan from the tropics,
monk-looking in borrowed woolen coat with hood,
hands in gloves. I'm falling in chaste love
with nun after nun who is back from overseas,
ready to retire from her gentle good works and toughness,
these sisters of charity who are
not wielders of rules and doctrines. Though . . .
they do forbid Sister Mary Assumption to
climb ladders anymore, as she is
turning one hundred this month.

Their snow-white heads glide
about the halls, float downstairs
nodding in friendliness, with passions seemingly eased,
transcendent, at lunch with me, voicing
radical political views with sweet smiles.

Don't Take the Subway Today

New York City's taxicabs and traffic,
horse hooves all clippety lickety Latin beat.
Where's the money clip, got change for a grand?
Elijah, go back to your cloud, quityabitchin,
you chose your own lifetime.

Try the Galaxy Café on West 46th Street.
Their coffee isn't a black hole, it
gets the ball, pitches it back quick. Be ready.

Cab driver and fare
yell at each other through partition,
a speed date while breaking the speed limit,
"Hey! There's Tina Fey!" right there on
7th and Houston. Two lifetimes, five minutes
link up, marry, break up,
faster than a fling.

All the winks of shopkeepers and servers,
 take the place of stars in a night sky.
"How you want your eggs, sweetie pie?"

Each day a fluid cast, regulars and pass throughs,
urban ecology of slush, spit, poop, oil, grease, smaze,
blue skies, gray skies, ska sounds from doorways,

pretzels, peanuts, hot dogs and tapas, tipsters, shell games,
twofers, scrawny trees, neon snakes,
brakes and gears, city music, electric connection,
shouts and horns, street adrenalin
kicking the ass of loneliness.

Travel Tales 13, A Shipboard Romance

    I.   Raven the Trickster

You're someone who likes to analyze everything, a friend
said to me, in a lilting voice
of acceptance of the world I questioned.

So I am shocked when a message appears in the air, a
thought too big for my head
like cartoon words in a balloon – her name in the air –
I must follow the orders of this imperative,
amazed at it.

Raven is giving me a gift. Raven, oh Raven,
it is not going to be easy, this gift.

    II. Yoga at the Concert

She tucks her crossed ankles
under her. Her knee lies on mine.
Happy yoga!

    III. The Nap

Lie here,
but don't keep me awake, I only had two hours of sleep.

Her breathing relaxes immediately, but mine . . .
I wonder if I even breathed,
lying still, hyper-aware, the line of touch,
revelation without explanation, knee, thigh,
stomach. Surely, I think, I cannot sleep,
but I do. The length of my body next to hers brings
both desire and peace.

   IV. Blessing

To show what a new romance
can stir up in the brain, just
knowing she was once
in a Christian cult brings me
to erupt in a thank you Jesus!
After lovemaking we slow dance naked in the cabin to
Sarah McLachlan singing "I Will Remember You."

   V. Endings

Sounds of engines change
as the ship slows to the port.
You know without announcement
leave-taking nears.

V. First Days Back

At home in Florida,
both are in my ears,
fjord echoes of Yukon wind whistling in
red cedar and
Florida palms clicking
in the warm breeze.
She is back to her home in the desert,
an unbreachable distance,
though the sunset here will roll west, and
I imagine her and the Joshua trees silhouetted
in this same light.

Afterwards

Still beneath my feet I feel the earth tremble,
roll of planet, goofy erratic tugs of moon.

Still acute the sense of cosmos, of fullness, levitation,
like the pleasant anarchy of an orchestra tuning up.

Not yet a breakfast of birdsong, not yet
knockings and tappings of friends,

not yet the return of land legs
that will grip ground and be

 less eager for dancing,
for walking on water.

Moving to Hollywood

one got a message

failed to get disciples

almost got a movie role

settled for a sourdough roll

one sought sunshine

couldn't get a shoeshine

one sought a chef job

offers up a blowjob

one sought a sex change

now seeks spare change

short on beach boys

bought a pound of white noise

learned how to snort coke

learned to eat an artichoke

one sought the absurd

embodied by the L word

glam glitter fashion

grove of lost passion

epic epiphany

provided by Tiffany

penance of whole grains

ambient migraines

even with the sunset

overdosed on kismet

Aging Wing Walker

Winding slowly around her,
swaddling safety jacket,
comfort zone shrinking.
She won't fly any more,
mentions terrorism at
the Boston marathon
she used to run. She
jokes she won't train for it
this year. Cities and sore feet,
or missing legs. Just when she
was having a good day.
Coffee upsets her stomach,
so she's dozing off more,
it's harder to get out at night.
Death won't be a wind sheer
fierce and fast, mean, carrying a scythe,
but sweet, patting her on the
head, turning down the music.
Way before the winding sheet,
she will ask to be wrapped
in a warm blanket.

Just a Second

Amid piles of past and little future, the shelves of unfinish,
even so, take the floating moment without action.

Along the highway, cotton tuft on hackberry thorn,
speared.
Closeted, a yellow shirt, never worn, forever fresh.

Someone arcs handfuls of cracked corn that separate,
spray out like fireworks, gently land.

The cranes eat a bite, then stop to preen,
chilling now, done with the hunger for awhile.

At Mumbai ghat dhobis hang bright saris
graceful beside clean white shirts.

Two prophets on the curb are trimming toenails.
Sounds of calling over rooftops, inscrutable as birdsong.

At first damp with dew, then the grass begins to dry.
On a taut, still arm, a damselfly.

Youth at the Gallery of Medieval Knights, New York Metropolitan Museum, 1960

If, on some blast of faith I might rely,

I'd heel and kneel before the cross, would burst

at last my armor that was first

a shield, then seemed a crypt, I would try.

Or thrust myself upon some spear to die,

to know at least a ravage of the cursed

held in last spasm, where fire's worst

impales on a deathless vision, the flaming eye.

      Whispers without voices, echoes in odorless air.

      Creation hangs upon a nail, as still

      as monuments. I reel, gasp to prove

my breath, where antique knights with vacant stare

      forever hold their noble pose. Chill

      metal shells that wait, and do not move.

Atlas on the Cruise Ship Ryndam

Fourteen decks piled high like a layer cake
too rich, too sweet. Few choose stairs over elevators.
Into the aft elevator enter four workmen
followed by two heavy women,
as another woman mutters, "I'll wait," and steps out.

The ship offers pampering in all directions,
towels shaped into tropical animals,
dining staff unfolding napkins, dropping them
into our laps.

Some vacationers cultivate a sense
of abundance.
Many overeat. "An average cruiser
gains a pound or two a day," the brochure
announces, not as though it were a poker win,
but certainly without judgment.

Other passengers sharpen their paranoia as plumbing
malfunctions, mysterious leaks cause mold
reaction from several sodden stateroom carpets.

The staff have many answers, though not
necessarily to the questions asked. It could be

vocabulary issues, a language barrier,
in this country and that, living forward and aft.

In the library, a huge book, an atlas attached to a stand
that turns, its two-foot pages offering global graphics,
maps, keys, charts, bits of history, stories of skirmishes
to be consumed and shared at tables along with radishes,
squashes carved into flowers.

The New York Times, condensed into
two well-written pages, is enough news to go with
such announcements as "Cruisers of the Ryndam, weather
forces us to cancel shore leaves. You will stay on board
and may enjoy the library, bingo, a cooking
demonstration."

As we passengers wobble and tip in the storm,
as coffees and cocktails spill,
the atlas on its pedestal is one thing here
staying securely balanced.

Beachdaze – do wah, de water, do whatcha like

it's night when the sparks start, stars fly,
at the buckle the bucket of water passes
hand to hand, over the sand, dances foot
to foot to put out the fire

in the morning, the snow-capped clouds roll in
sous chefs in white caps
mounds of slide, glide, tumble and tide
sh sh sh she rode she rode
shush shush do wah

it's noon on the stoop, walking on the green line
bandana cabana on the dike, secret crush
in the surf curl rush,
waves in wind set clothes to dry, rain to the sky –
hanging out, hanging five

hula dancers in the dunes
singing lazy tunes, read their runes
don't go back to work
shirk honey shirk, drying that shirt
is plenty work

voices of the sea mesmerize the mermaids
making a friend in the longest swim
the guitar player puts a handle on the sand barre,
knocks at the door of the sandal castle
true enough to win free lodging

clarinet cloud blows over the land
draws blue shades over the eyes of beach
and sets blue notes on its sunburned knows,
playing with the cymbals, playing the traps
shush shush shush do wah

Detroit behind the Eight Ball

- - for my first car, the Renault bought on Detroit's Magic Mile, and Michael Moore

Spare change jingles in my pocket,

men toss theirs in the parking lot.

Even that kind of change can be too much.

Water and air reach in concrete

pockets to get to steel and crack

out seams of Ford plants and Chevy plants.

Water a foreign substance like

Toyota and Honda. Wind whistles through

broken windows, buildings

with falling walls.

Change calls the bank shots, auto-

motive force. Nothing holds still. We

roll and spin and spend while we can.

Mystic on the Tarmac

Opened my car door to see Buddha
lying on the rain wet parking lot
water spreading the prisms of oil to form
two shapes, one for the sitting body, legs folded,
one for the head and face.
I stare, unable to move.

I'm tempted to declare this grease smear
as sacred ground, at least to point it out:
Look! Look! It's the Buddha!

I hear the wise beautiful one before me saying,
Just take this gift to your heart, go on about
your shopping. It's no big deal. I'm everywhere,
especially on a rainy day.

Sea Lion Lines

During a recent past life regression,
I found out something that amazed me.
I wasn't a glamorous Egyptian queen or a pirate,
I was a sea lion.

So much is
becoming clear, like
how I bark
and bellow at tailgaters.
Holdover from those
old days lying on a rock barking
at a neighbor getting too close
and stinking like seaweed.

As a sea lion, I loved swimming in icy water,
wallowing, waddling, flopping
up on the rock,
feeling that delicious
warm sun on my hide.

I was content in that world until
a National Geographic photographer
came, left a magazine that showed me
there was more to life than slurping mussels.

I turned the pages with my flipper and saw
deserts, lakes, streams, elephants and otters until the
precious magazine disintegrated
in salt water and seal piss.

I freaked. I was losing my treasure. I needed
a new magazine. Determined, I left
the rocky coast, the only world I ever knew,
to join the Venice Beach
art colony.

Fast forward to a corner in Santa Monica
where I stood flagging down a taxi.

The cabbie stopped and groaned, *Oh no,*
a sea lion! Well it's a fare
and I've had stranger passengers.
Where to?

I plopped in. *Take me to a photography school.*
The cabbie had a better idea.
I'll take you to Metro Goldwyn Mayer. They've
got a lion roaring in the beginning of their films,
why not a sea lion barking?

So, to make a long story short, I'm now seen
barking at the beginning of small, independent films,
subsidiaries of MGM.

If someone tells you your dreams are
all wet, just tell them to dry up. I have and, by God,
I'm famous.

Trip

A guy hovered over me eagerly as I sat on a bench,
recovering from my fall on the broken step,
"You could make them pay. I saw it all!"

"Nah," I say, "I fall, I bounce like a baby."
"Don't say that," he advised.
"Say you're brain dead."

For a second, I took that personally.
His eyes glittered. The intimate exchange made
my girlfriend suspect he had a crush on me.

I wanted to get away from him. He was
too close. He looked so normal, I was
afraid he was about to say

something Republican. I did like
the specificity of his suggestion.
Not the usual options for injury,

not whiplash, or sprained shoulder,
or even cracked kneecap.
Just plain brain dead.

Arcade: Quarter in Hand I Approach Her

Behind the glass case
the breast of the white-haired
fortune-teller heaves
as she breathes, lifting
her amber necklace.

"Don't you want to be free
instead of caged?" I ask.
She chuckles, her proper blouse
with lace ruffles almost
popping a button.

"Dear, I'm fine;
I always wanted to work in
an arcade. Now,
do you want your fortune?"

"Yes, Yes," I say.

"After your death, you
shall come back to life
as a juke box getting folks
loose with ragtime,
lots of Scott Joplin,
get people jumping."

"Me?"

"That's what I see, sweetie,
you'll make music like Joplin,
unearthly overtones,
whacked out music, make
happy for hard times."

Her breast stills.   I have no more quarters.
I hear rinky-tinky ragtime from the merry-go-round.

Visitor

In the beginning wafted in with bags of gifts,
sweaters over shoulders and arms, an ovoid of
cotton candy, about a foot off the ground.

In the middle landed loudly
with a belch and adenoidal critiques
of the settee's veneer,
the supposedly rancid salad oil,
the dog hairs on the davenport, the shelves
of despised authors.

In the end disappeared in a cloud of fumes,
leaving trenches of disparagement, leaves trod into dirt,
and into our minds, which admittedly had become
less and less innocent and lovely.

In the new beginning, we were frightened
and latched the gate.

Memoir from the Revolution

Memoir from the Revolution

Darkened sky at the hour of sunset
thunder today instead of molting golds,

the loneliness of the hour less
somehow, with rain hanging close by.

A memory of a screen porch with John Lee Hooker's
blues, day-long water coloring,

wine in mason jars, smokes,
one lover or another.

Later in the evening we played with a green tin top
dug into the Persian rug with each push and spin.

We almost saw, along with the utopias we were
dreaming up, time's unraveling.

How to Stop Fascism

To humans the elephant seems to move
slow as a wall, mud-caked tail a pendulum
marking a southern pace---
back and forth, ma'am, easy does it, ma'am.

But I on the beach unleashed, rushing the sandpipers,
kicking up sand, why, to sandpipers, I am
slow. They gossip "Who are those humans
thinking they can catch us?"

Time, is, after all, relative. Watch the
cup fall so slow its spoon floats in air
coffee glides out of the cup on a wide trail
like a meteor long in the sky— plenty slow,

plenty of watching time, plenty of dodging time.
We can watch a baseball leave the pitcher's hand
stretch the time of trajectory, move the bat to it easily.
We see fascism coming; watch it spin in the air.

We pray for a time warp of absolute focus, for
concentration we need to stop this, to hit it

bravely, square on, dissolve it out of the park,
round our bases and come home.

Alabama, 1961

The maid and I stood
on the green and white
squares of linoleum tile
beside the green plastic counter.
This was shiny and rich to me
when I gave up a fancy school
so my family could buy this house.
It was a neighborhood of the up-and-coming,
now mostly black,
a neighborhood of white trimmed brick
and white flight
and green lawns, but no garages or sidewalks.
We had all left our frame cottages and apartments
for the suburban middle class.
Trying to start a conversation, I said
I'd like to be a freedom rider.
Our pretenses imploded, our
identities shocked into new realities.
She never came back.
Our neighborhood turned a picture book page
neither of us could turn back.

Oh to Iron Out the Ironies

that games have winners and heartache
that scared democracies use torture
that I am heartless sometimes

that nature incinerates thousands without a qualm
that wars incinerate thousands without a qualm

that the healing air is barely sniffed
that the healing waters are rarely drunk

that as many suffer from too much as too little
that dreams are often more honest than rational minds

as to ironing, don't
clothes do just as well with a good shake
lordess! give us a good shake!

Year of Strong Storms

I think my house is in order
until a car passes playing
country music,
and in my house, all the tiny
objects vibrate,
forks in drawers, filaments
in light bulbs,
empty hangers pinging against
each other.

Chills crawl up my arms,
a narrow rim of tears circles my eyes.
Something in the earth is cracking.
My great aunt said, *Angels and devils*
will be fighting in the street,
it will be a horrible sight,
don't look out.

I think my house is in order,
and a wind comes by
loud as a train, and
my house gets on and rides

the wind out of town.

I'm waiting to see where it lands.

Evil Visible Again

TV screens, computer screens, pleas,
I can't breathe. Girl with phone that sees and hears
for us, a nation of witnesses sees and fears.

Knee on neck, zero respect, freeze, blood choke,
for nine minutes, nine centuries,
same old ropes on lynching trees.

Anger churns and unheard cries burn buildings,
glass shatters, garbage bins, maws of useless laws,
cracked jaws, cop claws.

Milky face of white bias, milky face in tear gas riot,
policeman's hand in pocket,
and socket of emptied heart locked.

A killer goes free, the suspect suffocates. Who
can take the right to breathe for granted? Not
the man in the paddy wagon, not

the terrible parade, one man shot in the back, one man
with skittles, one man who stole cigars, one man who sold cd's,
one man sold single cigs. Please!

One woman in her bed, wrong address, shot dead,
one man pulls out his license, not a gun,
on and on, adding one and one and one.

George Floyd was near a forgery.
Justice today is smeared and torn,
breathe and think, breathe and mourn.

Election

The election has tilted our house, our country,
so that people slide down a slope
to the side of the room full of rumors,
packed together in thick clouds of
loud lies that buzz like flies given birth in rot.

At these angles moderation is quashed, preservation,
conservation, nuance, as well,
and digging in only achieves splinters under fingernails,
no purchase gained.

In a utopia, after the election, I hope
opposing sides will level our mutual home,
let us sit in a circle with food and quiet talk.
(We can try forgiveness later, do something
easier now.) We can say,
tell us about a melody in you,
something you love.

Moment in Congress

When it is time, we can fail to speak our conscience.
We are flies in a web, must move lest regret be the spider,
capture us, snag the words we wish we had said.

Unsure how to weigh and balance
self-interest with justice, indecision
festers, calls in its cousins, adjusts
itself to evil, never apologizes
and life tipples its
poisons.

We get smaller
hoping to escape,
sneak through
the dilemma.

Our excuses swell
Against our skulls,
and to relieve the pressure
integrity must
shrink.

Vilano Beach

The dark streak of sky to the north,
only clue to a squall on the way.
We meanwhile sit happily under our cabana
observing those walking by---
the nearly nude, the belly bulging uncles, our favorite
ballerina-like shell collector always
retrieving each shell with a flourish, leaning down
with one leg up and toe pointed.
Screaming kids and seagulls are cued to come
by tossed bread bits, then scattered by
a dune buggy full of a loud crowd of the uncool
waving at us cheerily eluding our judgments.
Dogs winsomely sniff each other's
butts, and a young Lab lays a stick
by a woman's thin legs.

Two old ladies are overheard talking about mushrooms.

Is this a good day?
So long as the storm stays away, a good day
to enjoy this brief community.

Secrets of Success

Monkey tries to get the milkshake
by sticking the straw in the opening at the top,
pulling it out and licking it. Laborious,
until she thinks, takes a suck,
(having in her childhood, of course, known nipples) .
Envious monkeys notice and adopt her method.

Bombardier beetle having seen its siblings
disappear forever early in the night,
waits until the blood source has been snoring awhile,
then comes out of hiding under the pillow
to plunge in its straw and get some hefty draughts
without awakening its victim, and heads back to hiding.

Raccoon, caught too many times at the cat bowl on the
porch, learns to postpone eating and
darts off with the whole bowl.

And instead of waiting for lower taxes and smaller
government, Halliburton contractors and armament
manufacturers start wars and
suck the treasury dry.

Politics and the Little People

Pulling home around us like a shawl
Not waving campaign signs in the park
It won't be a brawl
Nor a lark

Sounds of people honking horns nearby
Withdrawn here willing to play scrooge
Feeling wary and shy
In this refuge

Balloon vines festive turkey tangle frogfruit
Indifferent to alligator and wild hog root
We hunker, stay put
Eat mango fruit

Like an elfin party for a birthday
Agaricacaes mushrooms tiny umbrellas
Little people at play
Merry fellas

Then at last, we act as we were asked
Brace to face the fingers and heckles

Up for the task
daring and reckless

We charge out with signs in drenching rain
The wee folks praise in wonder
When those giants speak
They thunder

Covid Cancellation

The hundred-year celebration of women's right to vote
was set, a calendar of joyous boxes ready to be filled,
but ready boxes gaped and chilled
and postponed plans grew moldy.
No plays, parades, no rally
rich with song and pride. The hollowed space
would populate with phantoms, the calendar rent,
dissolved events to empty rooms.

And too, triumphal travel set aside, even
plans for coastal camping now denied.
That cliff, those rocks, the pocking sounds
of surf in caves, left alone, the moan of moonset
heading toward the sea were not where
we would be. Unexpected viral specters, casual wrecks
instead began to loom, future foundered,
reset itself, to brace for any new erase.

Shutdown Carnegie Hall and other Caverns

Rows of empty theatre seats
hungry arms long for soft bodies.
Remembered faces blur
like clouds of underwater algae,
bare grocery shelves shiver and rattle
with labels laughing, ho ho holes,
wicked jokesters, offering only
hollow boasts of paper goods,
baking needs, coffee -- barren
dystopian echoes.

We work to morph words,
to banter rather than to bicker.
It's a time for a first soufflé,
for growing eggplants, for a schedule,
bass practice, sock feet salsa.

Our stage will be
our living room, we will be understudies
of the fire opal where, in its confined
space, colors dance and swirl.

Lost Parties

Parties left only echoing memories.
Thirty or so voices in the tree leaves still rustle and whistle.
Now we have nostalgia for those
kettle drums of feet up the long ramp, those
jokes about our aging popping knees sounding
like woodpeckers, dum tiddly dum,
with emphasis on the anapest.

In those rapturously loud old parties
 we cupped our ears to hear
over the noisy hurly burly of excited voices.
Music was wine and smoke
and singing with an invisible hymnal.
Those old parties only had quiet
when food was served.

After the Protest

I wake up from a nap as the protesters arrive,
a small group to decompress and gauge success,
one voice I don't know. I join the group in a
daze, welcomed as though I were a guest.

My friends who know their way around
my kitchen set out ice and silver, nuts and cheese.
The party crasher asks a few questions,
looks at mementos and refrigerator magnets,
leaves after awhile. No one knows what to make of him.
Someone says he was at the demonstration.

Later, a few of us sit on the dark porch
watching great bolts of lightning, between
bursts of thunder, as we swap stories of danger,
a sign snapped in two, batons on heads,
zipties and arrests, eyes burning with tear gas.

The stranger gone, we're relaxed for now.
The storm has passed though
the whole sky still lights up and the far horizon pulses.

Early in the Virus Years

A plumbing leak under
the kitchen sink soaked
four new paper towel rolls.
Ordinarily we'd toss them, but
we're hoping to dry them
out of their sodden state
because paper towels
can be as priceless as
Marco Polo's silk, like
toilet paper these days,
or rubbing alcohol for
homemade sanitizers, or
(I wish) LSD
for a higher consciousness.
We seldom can choose
our end of life. We can choose
a life, however short, of good cheer.
The whole country is punching
in on cell phones
no longer withheld I love you.
My spouse has ordered
a bidet and an ice cream maker.

Old resolutions
gain new strength.
I'm rowing daily on the lake.
Meanwhile the paper towels
are baking at 170 degrees, timer set,
turn them in 45 minutes.
We are communing despite isolation
with shared nuttiness,
abnormal the new normal.
Raise a sanitized hand if you agree!

Voices in the Chorus of Millions---2020

During months sheltering at home,
we've hacked through acres of thorns and
thickets of smilax to get out ardisia.

Laden with red berries, beautiful, aggressive,
obnoxious, invading oak hammocks, grabbing,
I'll take this, I'll take that. Hoarding
all land for itself, ardisia is snuffing out
other plants so deer can't pass, so mosses are
lost, so organic harmony collapses.
Even betony and violets surrender ground,
defenseless against unrelenting crowding.

Ardisia's ally, camphor, joins the encroachment,
opportunist leafy trees deflect sun,
an enemy of ardisia, sun that when
ardisia and camphor trees are gone, will drop
bright splashes of light through the canopy
to ease softly across the forest floor.

Our team is careful to stay
six feet apart, glad to find this work
restoring health to the woods.

We know that facing foot-grabbing vines,
ticks and chiggers,
spiders and snakes, snarls and cuts
doesn't make us heroic. In these days
when so many workers must risk death,
we sing the song we can.

Ancestors

I'm lying on a blanket on sparsely grassed sand near
the lake, warm in the sun yet still winter.

It has been so long since I have felt the ground beneath
my body, I'm wanting to feel its life and the life of its past
inhabitants as I gaze at these sparkling waters.

I wonder about the Timucuans who tried to adapt
to the white men's ways, and thrived for a while, only
to be gone now, with no descendants.

I've read about their tattooed skin,
their imposing heights, their system of trading
inland trout for coastal oysters.

I think of Dauphin Island where women of the
first people came from around the continent, ignoring
tribal enmities to share herbs and herbal cures.

Pottery from those far-flung groups
were found in grave sites along with one woman buried in
a chief's regalia.

I think of how this lake links with all rivers and springs
and portages, and how women came from here
to make the long journey to the gathering.

I think of how much less pollution there was, how many
more species before Europeans came. I press my ear
close to the ground, and close my eyes, praying to Earth

to hear her, to stay close to her, to be grateful
for all, from little bog button flowers to the trees'
highest canopies, the towering clouds and beyond.

Our, a Love Poem for Humanity

the person one arm white, one arm black
one side of face woman one side man
the head with front of curl back straight braid
the teeth of every color the nose breathing fire
the eyes flashing brown and blue
the aura orange and yellow,
the voice bass and falsetto, the hum alto, the song soprano,
the tenor thinking, the words dancing
the knees bending and kicking and creaking and stepping,
the shins shining, the elbow flying and waving
the hand playing and swaying

this is me this is you this is both of us this is our brother
this is our grandmother this is our child this is our childlessness,
these our adopted children
these are the schoolchildren
these are the hungry children being fed children,
these are the children who like to dress up,
these are the parents who like to dress down
these are the motley the clothes we found in each other's closets
these are the foods we've cooked for each other,
these avocados these grapes of glory wafers of water lilies,

god and goddess and will and wand protect us
occupy protect us holy basil tea protect us
lucid dreams protect us
music protect us love protect us
small rooms and wide sky protect us,
collards caress us, mushroom be our fortune,
stories be told us

we will know each other, we will go to strangers,
we will make homes for the homeless
we will give ourselves to partners to our friends to
everyone in our day to everyone along the way, we will work,
we will give hallelujahs
we will give unending thanks we will amen and om
we will be all modal music
we will sing all the songs never sung
we will address the morning the moon the sunset the shore
we will bring plums and oranges
we will bring flowers to our rivals,
we will fly with each other
we will lie down with each other in forever
we will listen and kiss forever

INDEX

A New Sunflower Species	15
A Pilgrimage to See Sister Maggie	102
After Mallarmé	53
After the Protest	145
Afterwards	109
Aging Wing Walker	111
Aging with You	85
Alabama, 1961	130
Ancestors	150
Anne Sexton Dream	69
Arcade: Quarter in Hand I	124
Approach Her Art After	68
Atlas on the Cruise Ship Ryndam	114
Beachdaze	116
Beware All-Consuming Passions	77
Big Island Ballet	10
Body Surfing	40
Break Out	89
Breakup in November	54
Brook Farms	14
Bye Sug	45
Cavern	16
Cold Snap	30
Couple Seeks Geographical Cure	42
Covid Cancellation	142
Detroit behind the Eight Ball	118
Divorce	46
Don't Take the Subway Today	104
Drought At Goldhead	95
Early in the Virus Years	146
Election	136
Evil Visible Again	134
Fog Song	2
Food of an Affair	34
Freeze Forecast in a Blue Moon	22
Greens of August	17
Gulf Island Ceremonial	6
Haiku	61
Holy Day USA	82
How to Stop Fascism	128
How to Tell if You're a Poet	94

I See You, But So What	18
I Want to Be Worthy: A Sermon for Self	74
Ichetucknee Canoe	12
In Love Again	57
Journal at Silver Glen Spring	4
Just a Second	112
Keeping Up Appearances	90
Kentucky Bourbon	36
Kissing Cousins	38
Lake Morning	13
Life on a Pedestal	67
Lost Parties	144
Memoir from the Revolution	127
Midsummer Night's Eve	51
Moment in Congress	137
Moving to Hollywood	110
My One and Only Poem to Charles Bukowski	70
Mystic on the Tarmac	119
Not Medusa	50
Ode to Heat	98
Oh to Iron Out the Ironies	131
Old Women and the Weeds	20
On the Verge	52
One Shoe	80
Our, a Love Poem for Humanity	152
Palaces of the Poor	92
Pi Day	83
Platonic	37
Poem for Pat	58
Poet at an Outdoor Restaurant	101
Politics and the Little People	140
Rash Diagnosis and Diogenes's Lamp	72
Ravine Ritual	24
Ripening	25
River Communities	5
Sailor's Farewell	47
Santa Fe Day	1
Saucerie	60
Sea Lion Lines	120
Secrets of Success	139
September Bardo	43

Shutdown Carnegie Hall	143	Trip	123
Silver Delicious	84	Triptych	66
Sleep Tight	79	Twelve	88
Solo Roads and the Single Girl	96	Untitled	33
Solstice and the Changing Seen	64	Valentine to a Poet	71
Speechless	8	Vernal Equinox	86
Sticking Points	48	Vespers	78
The Journals of Lost Brothers	81	Vilano Beach	138
The Point of Palms	63	Visitor	126
These Days with Us	56	Voices in the Chorus of Millions---2020	148
Three Generations Clearing Weeds	28	Vultures and Winter Rye	21
Time, You're a Rowdy Hag Like Me	76	Winter Dawn	23
Today's Tropical Adrenaline	19	Year of Strong Storms	132
Travel Tales 13, A Shipboard Romance	106	Yellow Fly Season	26
		Youth at the Gallery of Medieval Knights, New York Metropolitan Museum, 1960	113
		Zombie Love	44

www.ingramcontent.com/pod-product-compliance
Lightning Source LLC
Chambersburg PA
CBHW032119090426
42743CB00007B/396